THE UNVEILING OF THE MYSTERY OF INIQUITY

The Separation Between Religious Tradition and Truth About the Rapture

EUNICE SILVERNE FORCET

The Unveiling of the Mystery of Iniquity
Copyright © 2019 by Eunice Silverne Forcet

All Scripture quotations, unless otherwise
specified, are from The Holy Bible, King James
Version. Copyright © 2002 by Zondervan.

Tellwell Talent
www.tellwell.ca

ISBN
978-0-2288-2081-9 (Paperback)

Dedication

This book is dedicated to all of those in Christ who are anxiously waiting for the perfection of the Church, that long–awaited *kairos* moment when we will be full of the fullness of Christ, our hope of Glory, operating in the greater works and being made ready for the Day of the Lord.

Acknowledgements

I give thanks to my Lord and Savior Jesus Christ who considered me worthy to entrust with the task of writing this book revealing the mystery that has been kept hidden for ages and generations but is now disclosed to the Lord's people *(Col.1:26).*

> *And I heard, but I understood not: then said I, O my Lord, what shall be the end of these things? And he said, go thy way, Daniel: for the words are closed up and sealed till the time of the end. Many shall be purified, and made white, and tried; but the wicked shall do wickedly: and none of the wicked shall understand; but the wise shall understand (Dan. 12:8–10).*

Table of Contents

Dedication...iii

Acknowledgements iv

Introduction...vii

Part 1: The CLEANSING of the Church............................1

Part 2: Is the end-time Tribulation Period
        the wrath of God?..29

Part 3: The timeline of the DAY of the Lord....................35

Afterword 50

Notes 52

About The Author 53

Introduction

Now after the death of Moses, the servant of the Lord, it came to pass, that the Lord spake unto Joshua the son of Nun, Moses' minister, saying, Moses my servant is dead; now therefore arise, go over this Jordan, thou, and all this people, unto the land which I do give to them, even to the children of Israel (Jos. 1:1–2).

And Joshua rose early in the morning; and they removed from Shittim, and came to the Jordan, he and all the children of Israel, and lodged there before they passed over. And it came to pass after three days that the officers went through the host; and they commanded the people saying: "When you see the ark of the covenant of the Lord your God and the priests the Levites bearing it then you shall remove from your place and go after it. Yet there shall be a space between you and it about two thousand cubits by measure: come not near unto it that you may know the way by which you must go, for you have not passed this way heretofore" (Jos. 3:1–4).

Now is the time for the long-awaited *kairos* moment of the crossing over of the Church into her promised land from spiritual darkness, into the glorious light of the truth of the Word of God, the fullness of Christ in us, our hope of glory. We have not passed this way before.

Just like the children of Israel, the Church has been wandering about in a wilderness, unable to come to the full knowledge of the truth of the Word of God and to receive all His promises.

This was being allowed to happen by God as it was not yet the appointed time for this mystery, concealed throughout the ages, to be revealed. It was meant only for the end-time saints, as it was the Lord's sovereign will that the Church should not attain to this fullness until the end of the age in preparation for the Day of the Lord.

These misunderstandings of the Scriptures: false doctrines, false prophets, various denominations and all forms of counterfeit Christianity which have existed since the end of the early Church, are not happening by chance. There is a powerful, supernatural force a false antichrist spirit, a Mystery of Iniquity who is responsible for all of this. It was being allowed to function undetected in the Church until the appointed time for it to be revealed *(2 Thess. 2:4–6)*.

According to *2 Thessalonians 2:8*, when this entity is revealed, it shall be destroyed by the spirit of His mouth and shall be consumed by the brightness of His coming. It shall be destroyed when it is revealed, according to the Scriptures.

The Church, no longer being influenced by this Mystery of Iniquity, will enter into the fullness of Christ in us, our hope of glory, ready to do the greater works and be prepared for the Day of the Lord.

Through mistranslations, resulting in the misinterpretations of the Scriptures, this truth was kept hidden until now the time of the end, which is the appointed time for its revelation.

> *And I heard, but I understood not: then said I, O my Lord, what shall be the end of these things? And he said, go thy way, Daniel: for the words are closed up and sealed till the time of the end. Many shall be purified, and made white, and tried; but the wicked shall do wickedly: and none of the wicked shall understand; but the wise shall understand (Dan. 12:8–10).*

PART ONE

The CLEANSING of the Church

As the rain and the snow come down from heaven, and do not return to it without watering the earth and making it bud and flourish, so that it yields seed for the sower and bread for the eater, so is my word that goes out of my mouth: it will not return to me empty, but will accomplish what I desire and achieve the purpose for which I sent it (Isa. 55:10, 11).

Jesus is going to cleanse His Church. This is His promise to us that will not go back to Him void but will accomplish what He desires and will achieve the purpose for which He has sent it.

Now is the time when all the religious traditions of the past will be replaced by the truth of the Word of God. We are now at that long-awaited *kairos* moment for the Church, making way for the crossing over into a greater revelation of Christ in us, our hope of Glory.

Who now rejoice in my sufferings for you, and fill up that which is behind of the afflictions of Christ in my

> *flesh for His body's sake, which is His Church. Even the mystery which hath been hid from ages and from generations, but now is made manifest to His saints. To whom God would make known what is the riches of the glory of this mystery among the gentiles; which is Christ in you, the Hope of Glory (Col. 1:24, 26–27.)*

The mystery of the "Man of Sin" which has been hidden for ages and generations is now being revealed, allowing us to attain to our glorious hope, the fullness of Christ in us, which must occur before the Day of the Lord.

Traditionally, the glorious hope was purported to be the rapture of the Church before the start of the Tribulation Period. The basis for this was the belief that "we were not appointed to wrath." *Part 2* of this booklet elaborates on this topic and makes a case for what is truly meant by "our glorious hope."

Sometimes in the Bible, misinterpretations and mistranslations to the smallest degree can cause a text to be taken out of context, causing confusion, as was the case with the apostle Paul's teaching in *2 Thessalonians 2:1–8*. But then, at God's sovereign will, the true light of the meaning will shine forth and God's will will be done. He will accomplish what His set plan was even before the foundation of the world, the cleansing of His Church before that great and terrible Day of the Lord.

> *Immediately after the tribulation of those days shall the sun be darkened, and the moon shall not give her light, and the stars shall fall from heaven, and the powers of the heavens shall be shaken: And then shall appear the sign of the Son of man in heaven: and then shall all the tribes of the earth mourn, and they shall see the Son of man coming in the clouds of heaven with power and great glory. And he shall send*

his angels with a great sound of a trumpet, and they
shall gather together his elect from the four winds, from
one end of heaven to the other (Matt. 24:29–31).

It can be seen from the above Scripture that the "Day of the Lord" is when Jesus appears in the clouds of Heaven with power and great glory to gather His elect out of the tribulation and take them back with Him: the rapture of the Church.

2 Thessalonians 2:1–8

Below is a careful examination of *2 Thessalonians 2:1-8* separating the long-held religious traditions from truth concerning the rapture, the "Day of the Lord."

2 Thessalonians 2:1–2

Now we beseech you, brethren, by the coming of our
Lord Jesus Christ, and by our gathering together
unto him, that ye be not soon shaken in mind, or be
troubled, neither by spirit nor by word, nor by letter as
from us, as that the day of Christ is at hand.

The apostle Paul was giving the Church a warning that they should not be deceived, as they were concerned that the Day of the Lord had taken place. He then gave them a list of things which must occur before this can happen, as shown below:

2 Thessalonians 2:3a

Let no man deceive you by any means for that day
shall not come except there comes a falling away first.

There have been various discussions regarding the translation of the Greek word *apostasia* as "falling away." According to religious tradition, it is believed that this translation refers to the apostasy or falling away of the Church from the truth that must occur before the Day of the Lord. Others hold the belief that the proper translation should be "departure," as the Greek word *apostasia* is derived from *apo*, which means "from," and *istemi*, which means "stand"; therefore, the meaning of "to stand from" indicates a physical departure of something from somewhere. Traditionally, this was interpreted as being the departure of the Church in a secret rapture. "Departure" as being the correct translation is backed up by many scholars as earlier versions of the Bible, prior to the King James translation, used the word "departure," and not "falling away."

> *The first seven English translations of "apostasia" all rendered the noun as "departure" or "departing." They are as follows: Wycliffe Bible (1384); Tyndale Bible (1526); Coverdale Bible (1535); Cranmer Bible (1539); Breeches Bible (1576); Beza Bible (1583) and Geneva Bible (1608). This supports the notion that the word truly means "departure". The King James Version of the bible (1611) was the first to use "falling away" instead of the established translation of "departure".*[1]

This mistranslation has been accepted by Christians over many centuries and is now firmly established in Christian doctrine that a "falling away" of the Church to the antichrist must occur before the Lord can return. This error, through a mistranslation, has greatly affected the Church who has believed for centuries that a falling away must occur Silverne the Lord can return.

To verify this "falling away" theory, *1 Timothy 4:1* is often used; however, upon reading the whole chapter it would be found that this Scripture is a teaching from the apostle Paul to Timothy, in order to "save thyself, and them that hear thee" from falling away.

> *Now the Spirit speaketh expressly, that in the latter times some shall depart from the faith, giving heed to seducing spirits, and doctrines of devils. Take heed unto thyself, and unto the doctrine; continue in them: for in doing this thou shalt both save thyself, and them that hear thee (1 Tim.4:1, 16).*

Putting the above Scripture in context, the apostle Paul did not at all mean that a "falling away" of the Church *must occur* before the Lord can return; what was said was that in the latter times some shall depart from the faith … of devils. His teaching was meant to warn the true Church so that *they would not depart* from sound doctrine.

The Scriptures below show that those who would fall away to the antichrist are those whose names are not written in the Book of Life before the foundation of the world. The true children of God, whose names are written in the Book of Life, are not the ones who will fall away to the antichrist.

> *(1) And all that dwell upon the earth shall worship him, whose names are not written in the book of life of the Lamb slain from the foundation of the world (Rev. 13:8).*

> *(2) The beast that thou sawest was, and is not; and shall ascend out of the bottomless pit, and go into perdition: and they that dwell on the earth shall wonder, whose names were not written in the book of life from the foundation of the world, when they behold the beast that was, and is not, and yet is (Rev. 17:8).*

There are many instances in Scripture that also disprove this theory, as God's promises are in total contradiction to this tradition as it speaks of the restoration of the Church before the great and terrible Day of the Lord. *Joel 2:23–29; Isa. 28:15–18,*

60:1, 2; *Jn.17:25, 26; Col. 1:24, 26–27;* and *1Cor. 13:8–10, 12* all indicate that the Church will be perfected.

What must occur before the Lord can return is the perfection of the Church. This perfection of the Church with the fullness of Christ in us is what will usher in the great end-time harvest which will be the sign of the end.

The Scriptures below show that there are three levels of the spreading of the Gospel.

> *(1) And the gospel must first be published among all nations (Mark 13:10).*

> *(2) And He said to them: "Go into all the world and preach the gospel to every creature. He that believeth and is baptised shall be saved; but he that believeth not shall be damned (Mark 16: 15-16).*

> *(3) And this gospel of the Kingdom shall be preached in all the world for a witness unto all nations and then the end will come (Matt: 24:14).*

In the above Scripture Jesus told his disciples that the sign of the end will be when the Gospel is preached among all ethnic groups for a witness to them of the power and authority of the Lord.

The restored Church will now be operating in the fullness of Christ with great signs and wonders following, giving rise to the greatest ingathering of souls into the Kingdom of God.

This will not be done exclusively through evangelizing but by all Christians in every ethnic group who will be full of the fullness of the Holy Spirit doing miracles, signs, and wonders.

The Departure

It is a very well-known fact that the pre-tribulationists' view of "departure" is the departing of the Church in a secret rapture before the Tribulation Period; however, this viewpoint cannot be substantiated as there is definite proof that the tribulation saints will be going through a part of the Tribulation Period (see *Part 3, The Timeline of the Day of the Lord*).

These are all speculative conjectures resulting from religious tradition. Now the question remains: to what is "the departure" referring?

Strong's Concordance #646 gives the meaning of *apostasia* as "defection, revolt against," and HELPS Word Studies as "a leaving from a previous standing." It will be shown here what will be the "defection," or "revolt against" and from what "previous standing."

2 Thessalonians 2:3b, 4

> *And that man of sin be revealed, the son of perdition;*
> *who opposeth and exalteth himself above all that is called*
> *God, or that is worshipped; so that he as God sitteth*
> *in the temple of God, showing himself that he is God.*

The pre-tribulationists also believe that when the Church departs before the start of the Tribulation Period that the Holy Spirit, who is the restrainer preventing the Man of Sin from being revealed, also would depart from the earth allowing the identity of the human antichrist king to be revealed. He will then have free reign to do evil and blaspheme God. This is how he is described:

> *And the king shall do according to his will; and he*
> *shall exalt himself and magnify himself above every*
> *god, and shall speak marvelous things against the*
> *God of gods, and shall prosper till the indignation*
> *be accomplished: for that is determined to be done*
> *(Dan. 11:36).*

The antichrist king of the New World Order (NWO), who is being referred to above, is not the Man of Sin to whom the apostle Paul was referring in *2 Thess. 3b, 4.* This entity will not be destroyed when it is revealed but will accomplish the work for which it was predestinated. The Apostle was referring to an evil, antichrist spirit operating in the Church that remained a mystery to them.

> *Little children, it is the last time: and as ye have heard that antichrist shall come, even now are there many antichrists; whereby we know that it is the last time (1John 2:18)*

> *And every spirit that confesseth not that Jesus Christ is come in the flesh is not of God: and this is the spirit of antichrist, whereof ye have heard that it should come; and even now already is it in the world (1 John 4:3).*

> *For many deceivers are entered into the world, who confess not that Jesus Christ is come in the flesh. This is a deceiver and an antichrist (2 John 1:7).*

This antichrist spirit was also the cause of false prophets who were functioning in the churches: *Matt. 7:15; 24:11, 24; Mark 13:22; Luke 6:26; 2 Pet. 2:1.* From this it can be shown that the early Christians knew and recognized the Man of Sin as a satanic, antichrist spirit. The translators of the King James Bible in their letter to King James stated:

> *Manifesting ... by writing in defense of the truth (which had given such a blow unto that man of sin, as will not be healed).*[2]

The writing of this version of the Bible in "defense of the truth" could not have dealt a blow to the human antichrist king of the New World Order; obviously, they were referring to this antichrist spirit as the Man of Sin.

This antichrist spirit, is now sitting in the temple of God, the body of worshippers, and being worshipped as God causing all the deceptions, errors in doctrine, and falsifying of truth.

This counterfeit Christianity generated by this antichrist spirit still works in the Church today and will continue until it is taken out of her midst at the time appointed for the perfection of the Church.

By substituting the human antichrist king of the NWO for the antichrist spirit Man of Sin, the Church is being deceived into believing that there is no need for it to be cleansed from the working of this satanic entity as its focus is on the revelation of the identity of the human antichrist king of the NWO.

It was also believed that the temple (Greek *naos*) referred to the future temple to be established in Jerusalem during the reign of the human antichrist king; however, *naos* always has been used to indicate the corporate Body of Christ as the temple of God, as shown in many of the epistles, including: *1Cor. 3:16, 17; 6:19; 2 Cor. 6:16–17; Eph. 2:20–22;* and *1Pet. 2:5.*

This Man of Sin was already sitting in the temple of God, the individual members of the Body of Christ as a false, antichrist spirit. The rebuilt temple refers therefore to the restored Church when she is filled with the fullness of God, the Holy Spirit without measure. The fulfillment of the promise of Christ in us, our hope of glory.

2 Thessalonians 2:5–7

> *Remember ye not, that when I was with you, I told you these things? And now you know what withholdeth that he might be revealed in his time. For the mystery of iniquity doth already work: only he who now letteth will let, until he be taken out of the way.*

In the above Scripture there has been some debate regarding the translation of the Greek *ginomai* as "taken out of the way." Other translations are: "to take place," "come into existence," "to arise" and "to come to pass".

In Strong's Concordance #1096, *ginomai* is translated as "to come into being, to happen, to become." The word *mesos*, translated "way," is defined in Strong's Concordance #3319 as: "middle, in the midst of, among and between."

By substituting the different translations of those two words, *ginomai* and *mesos* according to the Strong's Concordance, this passage would then read: "Remember ye not that when I was with you I told you these things?" And now you know that this Mystery of Iniquity, who was already at work "in the midst of the Church" (Strong's #3319), was being hidden until the appointed time for its manifestation.

The apostle Paul already had knowledge of the workings of this Mystery of Iniquity. Mystery: "something that is secret or impossible to understand"; iniquity: "gross immorality." He reminded the Thessalonians that he had told them about it on a previous occasion. They did not understand the cause of this gross immorality that existed in the Church, as it was hidden and meant to remain a mystery until the appointed time for its revelation.

Identity of the Man of Sin

As this Mystery of Iniquity is no longer being restrained from being revealed, now is the time for its identity to be disclosed. He is a spiritual antichrist man of sin. This man of sin is satan, the son of perdition, the god of this age who is the prince of the power of the air, the "spirit who now works in the sons of disobedience" *(2 Cor. 4:4; Eph. 2:2).*

He is the fallen Lucifer, son of the morning. He said in his heart, "I will ascend into Heaven, I will exalt my throne above the stars of God. I will sit also upon the mount of the congregation, in the sides of the north" *(Is. 14:13).*

He is the one who deceived Eve in the Garden of Eden (*Gen. 3:1–6*), and so brought about iniquity into God's creation. He is spoken about as the great dragon and will meet his end at the consummation of all things.

> *And the great dragon was cast out, that old serpent called the Devil, and Satan, which deceiveth the whole world: he was cast out into the earth, and his angels with him (Rev.12: 9).*

2 Thessalonians 2:8:

> *And then shall that Wicked be revealed, whom the Lord shall consume with the spirit of His mouth, and shall destroy with the brightness of His coming*

Now that the appointed time has come and the Man of Sin is revealed as the one operating in the midst of the Church as: that Wicked, the spiritual antichrist, Mystery of Iniquity he will be destroyed. All the falsifying of truth and errors in doctrine will be consumed by the true Word of God, the Spirit of the Lord's mouth, and be destroyed by the brightness of the coming of His Holy Spirit.

This outpouring of God's Spirit will dispel all the darkness from the midst of the Church. Satan's power and authority will be crushed. The Church will be perfected. This fire will cleanse and purify our spirits, minds, and hearts, consuming all iniquity so that we will be able to cross over into the promise of God, the fullness of Christ Himself. This revelation is the key that opens the door to the fullness of Christ in us, our hope of glory, and ushers in the Day of the Lord.

> *That he might sanctify and cleanse it with the washing of water by the word, that he might present it to*

himself a glorious church, not having spot, or wrinkle, or any such thing; but that it should be holy and without blemish (Eph.5:26, 27).

If this entity were the human antichrist Man of Sin it means that he will be destroyed once he is revealed. If the human antichrist Man of Sin is destroyed when he is revealed, then how can he accomplish his evil deeds as contained in Revelation 13:11–18 and Daniel 11:36–45?

Below is a commentary on this portion of Scripture by Adam Clarke, a British Theologian of the nineteenth century:

Whom the Lord shall consume – He shall blast him so, that he shall wither and die away; and this shall be done by the spirit of his mouth – the words of eternal life, the true doctrine of the doctrine of Jesus; this shall be the instrument used to destroy this man of sin: therefore it is evident his death will not be a sudden but a gradual one; because it is by the preaching of the truth that he is to be exposed, overthrown, and finally destroyed.

The brightness of His coming – This may refer to that full manifestation of the truth which had been obscured and kept under by the exaltation of this man of sin.[3]

The Glorious Church

Charity never faileth: but whether there be prophecies, they shall fail; whether there be tongues, they shall cease; whether there be knowledge, it shall vanish away. For we know in part, and we prophesy in part. But when that which is perfect is come, then that which is in part shall be done away. For now we see through a glass darkly; but then face to face: now I know in part: but then shall know even as also I am known (1Cor. 13:8–10, 12).

The apostle Paul foresaw a perfect Church for some time in the future which will be very different from the one that existed during the writing of his epistle to the Corinthians. Many did not quite understand this passage of Scripture and believed that this perfection would occur after earthly life. But now, by applying the truths contained here as predicting the perfecting of the Church before the Day of the Lord, this has become an earthly reality.

This is the time when we will no longer be seeing through a glass darkly, but we will know fully all things pertaining to the person of Jesus Christ and the glorious truth of His Gospel. This process is occurring already as many are receiving first-hand knowledge of the Kingdom of God and are communicating with Jesus, not through visions and dreams but face to face.

Satan and his cohorts will desperately try to attack the Church, as was his custom, but this time nothing will work. The Church in this glorious state of perfection will be just too much for him; he will no longer be able to defeat her. The revelation of this spiritual antichrist Man of Sin and its destruction from the midst of the Church will cause her to be restored into the fullness of Christ in us, our hope of glory. This is what must occur before the Lord can return.

And he shall send Jesus Christ, which before was preached unto you:

Whom the heaven must receive until the times of restitution of all things, which God hath spoken by the mouth of all his holy prophets since the world began (Acts 3:20–21).

Prophecies Regarding the Restoration of the Church

In the Book of Zechariah, chapter 4, there is an account of the prophet seeing a golden candlestick with a bowl on the top of it with seven lamps, and seven pipes attached to the seven lamps. There were also two olive trees, one on the right side and one on the left side. When Zechariah inquired of the angel what these were he answered, saying:

> *This is the word of the Lord unto Zerubbabel, saying, Not by might, nor by power, but by my spirit, saith the Lord of hosts. Who art thou, O great mountain? Before Zerubbabel thou shalt become a plain: and he shall bring forth the headstone thereof with shoutings, crying, Grace, grace unto it. Moreover the word of the Lord came unto me, saying, the hands of Zerubbabel have laid the foundation of this house; his hands shall also finish it; and thou shalt know that the Lord of hosts hath sent me unto you. For who hath despised the day of small things? for they shall rejoice, and shall see the plummet in the hand of Zerubbabel with those seven; they are the eyes of the Lord, which run to and fro through the whole earth. Then answered I, and said unto him, What are these two olive trees upon the right side of the candlestick and upon the left side thereof? And I answered again, and said unto him, What be these two olive branches which through the two golden pipes empty the golden oil out of themselves? And he answered me and said, Knowest thou not what these be? And I said, No, my lord. Then said he, these are the two anointed ones that stand by the Lord of the whole earth (Zech. 4:6–14).*

We again see in *Revelation 1:12–20* where the apostle John saw seven golden candlesticks:

And I turned to see the voice that spake with me. And being turned, I saw seven golden candlesticks; and in the midst of the seven candlesticks one like unto the Son of man, clothed with a garment down to the foot, and girt about the paps with a golden girdle. His head and his hairs were white like wool, as white as snow; and his eyes were as a flame of fire; and his feet like unto fine brass, as if they burned in a furnace; and his voice as the sound of many waters.

And he had in his right hand seven stars: and out of his mouth went a sharp two—edged sword: and his countenance was as the sun shineth in his strength. And when I saw him, I fell at his feet as dead. And he laid his right hand upon me, saying unto me, Fear not; I am the first and the last: I am he that liveth, and was dead; and, behold, I am alive for evermore, Amen; and have the keys of hell and of death. Write the things which thou hast seen, and the things which are, and the things which shall be hereafter; the mystery of the seven stars which thou sawest in my right hand, and the seven golden candlesticks. The seven stars are the angels of the seven churches: and the seven candlesticks which thou sawest are the seven churches (Rev.1:12–20)

Zechariah's vision can be correlated to *Revelation 1:12–20*, as it solves the mystery of the golden candlesticks as being the seven churches and verifies the cleansing of the Church by the spirit of God. As grace relates to the Church age, these prophecies can also be determined to be referring to the restoration of the Church by the destruction of the antichrist spirit from its midst by the grace of God.

The anointing that will be coming upon the Church in the end-time glory could very well be from the oil of the two anointed ones who stand by the Lord of the whole earth, and from whom the oil is being poured into the candlesticks.

These are purported to be Moses and Elijah. Both prophets performed the signs and wonders that are also to be the acts of the end-time Church: Moses, when he confronted the Pharaoh of Egypt *(Exodus 5–12)*, and Elijah, when he confronted the prophets of Baal *(1 Kings 18)*.

This great cleansing of the Church from the works of this Mystery of Iniquity was veiled, to be revealed only at the time of the end as Almighty God had declared to His servants the prophets.

> *And I will shake all nations, and the desire of all nations shall come: and I will fill this house with glory saith the Lord of Hosts. The glory of this latter house shall be greater than of the former, saith the Lord of Hosts: and in this place will I give peace saith the Lord of hosts (Haggai 2:7, 9).*

The following charts give a comparison between the characteristics and determined end of the antichrist spirit (Mystery of Iniquity) Man of Sin and that of the human antichrist king of the NWO Man of Sin, which show that they are two separate entities.

CHARACTERISTICS OF THE SPIRITUAL ANTICHRIST (MYSTERY OF INIQUITY) VS. CHARACTERISTICS OF THE FUTURE HUMAN ANTICHRIST KING OF THE NEW WORLD ORDER

SPIRITUAL ANTICHRIST (MYSTERY OF INIQUITY) CHARACTERISTICS	HUMAN ANTICHRIST KING OF THE NEW WORLD ORDER CHARACTERISTICS
2 Thess. 2:4: *He opposes and exalts himself above all that is called God, or that is worshipped; so that he as God sitteth in the temple of God showing himself that he is God.* 2 Thess. 2:7: *For the Mystery of Iniquity doth already work only he who now letteth will let until he be taken out of the way.* He was already at work in the Church at the time of Paul's writings, causing all of the falsifying of truth, errors in doctrine, and false prophets which still exist today.	Daniel 11:36–39 *And the king shall do according to his will; and he shall exalt himself, and magnify himself above every god, and shall speak marvelous things against the God of gods, and shall prosper till the indignation be accomplished: for that that is determined shall be done.* *Neither shall he regard the God of his fathers, nor the desire of women, nor regard any god: for he shall magnify himself above all.* *But in his estate shall he honor the God of forces: and a god whom his fathers knew not shall he honor with gold, and silver, and with precious stones, and pleasant things.* *Thus shall he do in the most strongholds with a strange god, whom he shall acknowledge and increase with glory: and he shall cause them to rule over many, and shall divide the land for gain.*

DESTRUCTION OF THE SPIRITUAL ANTICHRIST
VS.
DESTRUCTION OF THE FUTURE HUMAN ANTICHRIST KING OF THE NEW WORLD ORDER

SPIRITUAL ANTICHRIST DESTRUCTION	*HUMAN ANTICHRIST KING OF THE NWO DESTRUCTION*
2 Thess. 2:8: *And then shall that wicked be revealed, whom the Lord shall consume with the spirit of His mouth, and shall destroy with the brightness of His coming.* The spiritual antichrist or Mystery of Iniquity man of sin will be destroyed when he is revealed. This is when the spiritual darkness causing the falsifying of truth and errors in doctrine is removed from the midst of the Church by the consuming fire of the Spirit of the mouth of the Lord. This darkness will be consumed by the brightness of the light of the true gospel, bringing the Church into the fullness of Christ ready for her end–time glory. The above indicates the destruction of the antichrist spirit, Mystery of Iniquity from the midst of the Church.	Rev. 19:11: *And I saw heaven opened, and behold a white horse; and he that sat upon him was called Faithful and true and in righteousness he doth judge and make war.* Revelation 19:20: *And the beast was taken, and with him the false prophet that wrought miracles before him, with which he deceived them that had received the mark of the beast, and them that worshipped his image. These both were cast into the lake of fire burning with brimstone.* Daniel 7:11: *I beheld then because of the voice of the great words which the horn spake: I beheld even till the beast was slain, and his body destroyed, and given to the burning flame.* The above indicates the determined end of the antichrist king of the NWO.

How the Mystery of Iniquity Entered the Church

> *And there appeared a great wonder in heaven; a woman clothed with the sun, and the moon under her feet, and upon her head a crown of twelve stars: And she being with child cried, travailing in birth, and pained to be delivered. And there appeared another wonder in heaven; and behold a great red dragon, having seven heads and ten horns, and seven crowns upon his heads. And his tail drew the third part of the stars of heaven, and did cast them to the earth: and the dragon stood before the woman which was ready to be delivered, for to devour her child as soon as it was born. And she brought forth a man child, who was to rule all nations with a rod of iron: and her child was caught up unto God, and to his throne. And the woman fled into the wilderness, where she hath a place prepared of God, that they should feed her there a thousand two hundred and threescore days (Rev 12:1–6).*

The above Scripture gives a spiritual account of the great conflict that occurred to prevent the birthing of the Church. The Church was birthed through the nation of Israel, from the genealogy of Mary, a virgin conceived by the Holy Spirit *(Luke 1:26–33)*. There is evidence of this throughout the Old Testament that it was through the tribe of Judah that the Saviour would enter the world.

History shows that there were many attempts made to destroy the nation of Israel by many of the other kingdoms that were in existence at that time.

The great red dragon, having seven heads and ten horns and seven crowns upon his head, signifies the ruling government whose objective it was to destroy the nation of Israel and consequently destroy the plan of God for the birthing of the Church and the establishment of the new covenant.

They were all under the influence of the evil one and his cohorts who joined in with the rebellion. But the cries and pain of the ancients for the Saviour and deliverer of Israel were heard; his power and authority were defeated and the Saviour was born.

Soon after the birth of Jesus, the mediator of the new covenant, the ruling government of the day, led by Herod the Great and instigated by satan, sought to destroy the young child and in so doing massacred the innocents of Bethlehem and the surrounding area killing all of the male children of Jesus's generation.

Satan was in complete rebellion against this move of God to provide a sacrifice for sin. His kingdom was greatly threatened, as his power over the saints would be shattered. He was able to influence others to join him in this rebellion and they were all cast out. Fallen angels are among the evil spirits who are members of the kingdom of darkness and who roam the earth doing the bidding of their wicked master by persecuting the Church. However, because of Jesus's sacrifice for us on the Cross, they have power but no authority over us; therefore, they cannot overcome the children of God.

> *And they overcame him by the blood of the Lamb and*
> *by the word of their testimony; and they love not their*
> *lives unto death (Rev. 12:11).*

In spite of it all, the Church was formed and preserved by God. During the three-and-one-half years of the ministry of Jesus she was protected and the establishment of the Church on the earth was unhindered.

This did not continue. Some time after the death and resurrection of Jesus Christ, satan with subtlety infiltrated the

Church as the Mystery of Iniquity. He remained hidden, and was the cause of false doctrines, errors in doctrine, different denominations, cults and false prophets which have existed throughout Church history.

> *And when the dragon saw that he was cast unto the earth, he persecuted the woman which brought forth the man child And to the woman were given two wings of a great eagle, that she might fly into the wilderness, into her place, where she is nourished for a time, and times, and half a time, from the face of the serpent. And the serpent cast out of his mouth water as a flood after the woman, that he might cause her to be carried away of the flood. And the earth helped the woman, and the earth opened her mouth, and swallowed up the flood which the dragon cast out of his mouth (Rev. 12:13–16)*

In the above, we see the Church being protected for another three-and-one-half years, from satan's persecution, during the first half of the final seven years of the Tribulation Period. She will be in all her fullness just as Jesus was during the first three-and-one-half years of His ministry. She will be filled with the full measure of the Holy Spirit as was Jesus; a glorious witness to the whole world and especially to the Jews, who also will be restored at that time.

In *Matthew 13:24–30*, Jesus spoke a parable about the wheat and the tares. This shows that there is a satanic seed planted by the enemy in the midst of the Church who will be plucked up and burned at the time of the end.

Victory After Defeat for the Saints of God

At the end of the three-and-one-half years of victory, by God's sovereign will the Church will be given over into the hands of the antichrist government. But they will not prevail, as his dominion will be taken away and given to the saints of the Most High God.

> *And the dragon was wroth with the woman, and went to make war with the remnant of her seed, which keep the commandments of God, and have the testimony of Jesus Christ (Rev. 12:17).*

> *But the court shall be seated, and they shall take away his dominion, To consume and destroy it forever. Then the kingdom and dominion and the greatness of the kingdoms under the whole heaven, shall be given to the people, the saints of the Most High. His kingdom is an everlasting kingdom and all dominions shall serve and obey Him (Dan. 7:26–27).*

This is an account of how satan because of his anger and rebellion infiltrated the Church and remained hidden as the Mystery of Iniquity. Now that he is revealed he will be destroyed giving rise to the greatly anticipated end-time glory.

> *Many shall be purified, and made white, and tried; but the wicked shall do wickedly, and none of the wicked will understand, but the wise shall understand (Dan. 12:10)*

The Gradual Enlightenment of the Church

Throughout history, there were many reformations of the Church. Great men of God received enlightenments about certain errors in doctrines and traditional customs, but even now the Church is stilled plagued by false doctrines.

The year 2017 was the five hundredth anniversary of Martin Luther King and his 95 Theses that splintered Catholic Europe giving rise to the Protestant Reformation. Resistance to this movement in Germany with fifty-six respected Evangelical leaders signing the Berlin Declaration in 1909 created a massive backlash as it was thought to be the harbinger of WWI with all of its horrors.[4]

There were many others who discovered errors in doctrine and made corrections bringing enlightenments, such as: William Seymore, Smith Wigglesworth, John Wesley, Charles Parham (the 1906 Azuza Street Revival) and, more recently the Charismatic Movement in 1960 and many more modern-day revivals. None of them was able to come to the total fullness of the truth as the appointed time had not yet come for "that Wicked" to be revealed. The Mystery of Iniquity was still at work.

This deceiver is still working in the churches today. The early scholars did not understand the workings of this Mystery of Iniquity and attributed the corruptions in doctrine to a variety of causes such as: the Roman Empire; the Roman leaders Nero, King Constantine, Caesar, Caligula; the Papal Dynasty; Mahomet and many others but the real cause was that one satanic spirit, the Mystery of Iniquity.

All of the dissertations written about this topic, about who or what was the cause of these errors in doctrine and the falsifying of truth, can now be put to rest as it was the work of that ancient deceiver, whose sole aim even from the beginning of creation was to be worshipped as God. It was God's sovereign will to allow this Mystery of Iniquity to remain hidden as it was His plan for the Church to receive its ultimate perfection at the end of the age.

The Fullness of the Gentiles: the Restitution of Israel

According to religious tradition, the fullness of the Gentiles was thought to be after the last person appointed to receive salvation was converted. It is very important to interpret correctly the meaning of the fullness of the Gentiles: does it mean until the full number to be converted worldwide is completed or when the Church has reached to the fullness of Christ in us, our hope of glory?

The Greek word *pleroma* (Strong's #4138) means "fullness," a filling up, and always has been translated as such. It was never intended to mean the full complement of those who would receive salvation worldwide.

As it now has been revealed that what must occur before the Day of the Lord is the fullness of Christ in us, it easily can be seen that this is what is meant by the fullness of the Gentiles which will usher in the restitution of Israel.

In *Acts 3*, the apostle Paul, after the healing of the lame man, told those present it was because of Jesus the Messiah whom they had rejected that the healing had occurred. He also preached to the Jews that they should repent and be converted, and that a time of refreshing will come when Jesus will be sent among them again, upon the restitution of all things and the restoration of the Church.

> *Repent ye therefore, and be converted, that your sins may be blotted out, when the times of refreshing shall come from the presence of the Lord.*
>
> *And he shall send Jesus Christ, which before was preached unto you:*
>
> *Whom the heaven must receive until the times of restitution of all things, which God hath spoken by the mouth of all his holy prophets since the world began (Acts 3:19–21).*

When the Church is restored onto the foundation stone laid in Zion doing miracles and the greater works, this will cause Israel to believe that Jesus is truly the Messiah, and they will be grafted back into their own olive tree.

> *And they also, if they abide not still in unbelief, shall be grafted in: for God is able to graft them in again. For if thou wert cut out of the olive tree which is wild by nature, and wert grafted contrary to nature into a good olive tree: how much more shall these, which be the natural branches, be grafted into their own olive tree? For I would not, brethren, that ye should be ignorant of this mystery, lest ye should be wise in your own conceits; that blindness in part is happened to Israel, until the fullness of the Gentiles be come in. And so all Israel shall be saved: as it is written, there shall come out of Sion the Deliverer, and shall turn away ungodliness from Jacob: For this is my covenant unto them, when I shall take away their sins (Romans 11:23–27).*

The Iniquity of Israel Will Be Removed in One Day

> *For behold the stone that I have laid before Joshua; upon one stone shall be seven eyes: behold, I will engrave the graving thereof, saith the Lord of hosts, and I will remove the iniquity of that land in one day (Zech.3:9–10).*

We Will Both Become One New Man

> *For he is our peace, who hath made both one, and hath broken down the middle wall of partition between us; having abolished in his flesh the enmity, even the law of commandments contained in ordinances; for to*

make in himself of twain one new man, so making
peace; and that he might reconcile both unto God in
one body by the cross, having slain the enmity thereby:
and came and preached peace to you which were afar
off, and to them that were nigh. For through him we
both have access by one Spirit unto the Father. Now
therefore ye are no more strangers and foreigners, but
fellow citizens with the saints, and of the household
of God; and are built upon the foundation of the
apostles and prophets, Jesus Christ himself being the
chief corner stone (Eph. 2:14–20).

The Human Antichrist Leader, or the Beast of Revelation

The human antichrist leader, the beast of Revelation, will be possessed by the same satanic entity, the Mystery of Iniquity.

Zech. 5:5–11 gives a strange account of an ephah of iniquity that goes forth with a woman called wickedness sitting in its midst who was carried to "the land of Shinar" by two women with wings. A house was built for her there, where she was established and set upon her own base.

This false, wicked antichrist spirit, the Mystery of Iniquity, when it is taken out of the midst of the Church, will be carried away to be set up in the rebuilt Babylonian temple in Jerusalem which will be established during the Tribulation Period. It will be flanked by the false prophet and the human antichrist king whom it will embody and now become the human antichrist man of sin ruler of the NWO as referred to in the Scripture below.

Even him, whose coming is after the working of Satan
with all power and signs and lying wonders, And
with all deceivableness of unrighteousness in them that
perish; because they received not the love of the truth,
that they might be saved. And for this cause God shall

send them strong delusion, that they should believe a lie: that they all might be damned who believed not the truth, but had pleasure in unrighteousness (2 Thess. 2:9–11).

No longer hidden, but in open manifestation he will blaspheme the true God and the Lord Jesus (*Dan. 11:36–39*). He will be worshipped as God by all those whose names are not written in the Book of Life (*Rev. 13:8*).

Summary of Misinterpretations

The true meaning of *2 Thess. 2:1–8* was completely misinterpreted. It is a very important passage of Scripture, as it deals with information for the Church regarding the end times and what must occur before the Lord can return.

The errors in this passage of Scripture, as summarized below, show that there was a deceptive plot by the enemy to prevent the Church from being ready for the coming of the Lord and for it to be delayed. Traditions alone teach the following:

1. The mistranslation of *apostasia* as "falling away," or apostasy of the Church so that the Church would wait expectantly for such a falling away instead of anticipating the great perfecting of the Church.

During the reign of the antichrist it is not the Church but the world who would revolt against Christianity. The true children of God cannot fall away to the antichrist.

And all that dwell upon the earth shall worship him, whose names are not written in the book of life of the Lamb slain from the foundation of the world (Rev. 13:8).

2. Believing in a secret pre-tribulation rapture so that the Church would not be prepared to face the tribulation, and without the hope and expectation of being perfected, the Church will not be cleansed, preventing the return of the Lord.

3. The substitution of the revelation of the Man of Sin, for the revelation of the identity of the human antichrist king of the NWO so that this spiritual antichrist would remain hidden in the midst of the Church allowing the errors of doctrine and falsifying of truth to continue.

4. The fullness of the Gentiles as the full complement of those who will be converted worldwide instead of the spiritual fullness of Christ in His Church.

This deceiver was being allowed to operate within the Church by God for His own sovereign reason as these revelations were meant only for the end-time Church. It is now time for the captives to be set free for a great display of God's might and power ushering in the restitution of Israel and the Day of the Lord.

PART TWO

Is the end-time Tribulation Period the wrath of God?

Now we beseech you, brethren, by the coming of our Lord Jesus Christ, and by our gathering together unto him, that ye be not soon shaken in mind, or be troubled, neither by spirit nor by word, nor by letter as from us, as that the day of Christ is at hand (2 Thess. 2:1–2).

In the above Scripture, the apostle Paul is reassuring the Church at Thessalonica that they should not be worried that "the day of Christ" is at hand. To understand what the Apostle meant by that term, "the day of Christ," he also refers to it as the "coming of our Lord."

May the God of peace himself sanctify you completely, and may your whole spirit, soul and body be kept blameless at the coming of our Lord Jesus Christ. He who calls you is faithful; he will surely do it (1 Thess. 5:23–24).

The pre-tribulationists hold to the tradition that the promise of the rapture of the Church before the coming of the antichrist and the Tribulation Period is the blessed hope and joy of the Church, as they were "not appointed to wrath." Not being appointed to wrath seems to have formed the basis for this argument that the Church will be raptured before the start of the Tribulation Period which is viewed as being the wrath of God.

We are to examine the Scriptures to understand fully what is meant by "the wrath of God," and if the end-time Tribulation Period is the wrath of God, for whom is it intended?

> *But let us, who are of the day, be sober, putting on the breastplate of faith and love; and for an helmet, the hope of salvation. For God had not appointed us to wrath but to obtain salvation by our Lord Jesus Christ (1 Thess. 5:8, 9).*

The above passage of Scripture is used to emphasize that the Church was not appointed to wrath; however, it clearly shows that the opposite of being appointed to wrath is being appointed to salvation.

> *For the wrath of God is revealed from heaven against all ungodliness and unrighteousness of men, who hold the truth in unrighteousness (Rom. 1:18).*

> *Whoever believes in the son has eternal life; whoever does not obey the Son shall not see life, but the wrath of God remains on him (John 3:36).*

> *And if anyone's name was not found written in the book of life, he was thrown into the lake of fire (Rev. 20:15).*

If anyone does not abide in me he is thrown away like a branch and withers; and the branches are gathered, thrown into the fire, and burned (John 15:6).

But I will warn you whom to fear: fear him who, after he has killed, has authority to cast into hell. Yes, I tell you, fear him! (Lk.12:5).

What if God, desiring to show his wrath and to make known His power, has endured with much patience vessels of wrath prepared for destruction (Rom. 9:22).

For the wages of sin is death, but the free gift of God is eternal life in Christ Jesus our Lord (Rom. 6:23).

Truly, truly, I say to you, whoever hears my Word and believes him who sent me has eternal life. He does not come into judgment but has passed from death to life (Jn.5: 24).

In him we have redemption through his blood, the forgiveness of our trespasses, according to the riches of his grace (Eph. 1:7).

For God so loved the world, that he gave his only begotten Son, that whosoever believeth in Him should not perish, but have eternal life (Jn.3:16).

The Lord knows how to deliver the godly out of temptations and to reserve the unjust unto the day of judgment to be punished (2 Pet. 2:9).

By contrasting the above Scriptures, it clearly can be shown that the opposite of wrath is salvation, the redemption of our souls. We are possessors of that free gift of God: eternal life. Even if the saints do go through a portion of the Tribulation Period, they are not appointed to wrath; therefore, they will not be destroyed like the wicked but will obtain their salvation.

The wrath of God is the determined end of the wicked, whose names are not written in the Book of Life and who are reserved unto the Day of Judgment to be punished, as opposed to those who are appointed to salvation whose determined end is eternal life with God.

> *And I saw another sign in heaven, great and marvelous, seven angels having the seven last plagues; for in them is filled up the wrath of God. And I saw as it were a sea of glass mingled with fire: and them that had gotten the victory over the beast, and over his image, and over his mark, and over the number of his name, stand on the sea of glass, having the harps of God. And they sing the song of Moses the servant of God, and the song of the Lamb, saying, Great and marvelous are thy works, Lord God Almighty; just and true are thy ways, thou King of saints. Who shall not fear thee, O Lord, and glorify thy name? For thou only art holy: for all nations shall come and worship before thee; for thy judgments are made manifest. And after that I looked, and, behold, the temple of the tabernacle of the testimony in heaven was opened: And the seven angels came out of the temple, having the seven plagues, clothed in pure and white linen, and having their breasts girded with golden girdles. And one of the four beasts gave unto the seven angels seven golden vials full of the wrath of God, who liveth for ever and ever. And the temple was filled with smoke from the glory of God, and from his power; and no man was able to enter into the temple, till the seven plagues of the seven angels were fulfilled (Rev. 15:1–8).*

In the above passages of scripture, reference is made to those who had been victorious over the beast and his mark and are in Heaven standing on the sea of glass and having the harps of God indicating the coming of the Lord had occurred. It shows that the saints are in Heaven before the seven last plagues of the golden vials full of the wrath of God are released upon the earth.

In *Revelation 19:1–9*, there is great rejoicing in Heaven as the saints are safely home and are at the marriage supper of the Lamb. In contrast to *Revelation 19:11–21*, which shows the Lord and the armies of Heaven returning to earth and making war with the beast and the kings of the earth. This clearly shows the destruction of the wicked. They are those whose names were not written in the Book of Life and did not serve God, but the antichrist.

> *And all that dwell upon the earth shall worship him,*
> *whose names are not written in the book of life of the*
> *Lamb slain from the foundation of the world (Rev. 13:8).*

This is the wrath of God upon the wicked. From this, we see that the Church will experience a part of the Tribulation Period but will not be included in the judgment of the wicked. The rapture of the Church will be a pre-judgment rapture, the same as with Noah, and Lot. They endured and lived through the difficult Tribulation Period of their time but were rescued just before the judgment of God upon the wicked.

PART THREE

The timeline of the DAY of the Lord

The following are some of the events that Jesus said will signify His coming and the end of the world. It also shows the fate of the Christians during that time.

And as He sat upon the Mount of Olives, the disciples came unto him privately, saying: Tell us when shall these things be? And what shall be the sign of thy coming and of the end of the world? (Mt. 24:3).

Then shall they deliver you up to be afflicted and shall kill you: and ye shall be hated of all nations for my name's sake (Mt. 24:9).

And except those days should be shortened, there should no flesh be saved: but for the elect's sake those days shall be shortened (Mt. 24:22).

Immediately after the tribulation of those days shall the sun be darkened, and the moon shall not give her light, and the stars shall fall from heaven, and the

> *powers of heaven shall be shaken: And then shall appear the sign of the Son of man in heaven: and then shall all of the tribes of the earth mourn, and they shall see the Son of man coming in the clouds of heaven with power and great glory. And He shall send His angels with a great sound of a trumpet, and they shall gather together His elect from the four winds, from one end of heaven to the other (Mt. 24:29–31).*

The above Scriptures show that the rapture will occur immediately after the tribulation of those days. From this it can be determined that "the tribulation of those days" refers to a certain portion of the Tribulation Period and not at the end of it; therefore, the major issue for consideration becomes during what part of the Tribulation Period will the Lord's coming occur.

There are contributory factors which prove that it is during the portion of the Tribulation Period between *Revelation 11:15*, the sounding of the last trumpet, and *Revelation 15:1*, the beginning of the seven last plagues filled up with the wrath of God, the vial judgments. All the signs leading up to the Day of the Lord are fulfilled in this portion of Scripture as indicated below:

- In *Revelation 11:15*, the last trumpet sounds: Jesus returns at the last trumpet.
- In *Revelation 14:6*, the Gospel is preached by an angel unto them who dwell on the earth, and to every nation and kindred, and tongue and people: this gospel of the kingdom shall be preached in all the earth and then the end will come.
- In *Revelation 14:15–20*, the earth is being reaped, for the harvest of the earth is ripe: Jesus returns at the end-time harvest.

- In *Revelation 15:2*, the saints who were victorious over the beast and his image, and over his mark, and over the number of his name stand on the sea of glass having the harps of God implying that the rapture had taken place. These were beheaded and were partakers of the first resurrection and are now standing in Heaven on the sea of glass, having the harps of God.

The above indicates that the Day of the Lord had taken place at this specific point during the Tribulation Period before the seven angels having the seven last plagues are commanded to pour out the vials of the wrath of God upon the earth.

It can be concluded, therefore, that the Lord's coming will occur before the beginning of the vial judgments and that the saints were present during the previous judgments.

> *And I saw as it were a sea of glass mingled with fire: and them that had gotten the victory over the beast, and over his image, and over his mark, and over the number of his name, stand on the sea of glass, having the harps of God. And they sing the song of Moses the servant of God, and the song of the Lamb, saying, Great and marvelous are thy works, Lord God Almighty; just and true are thy ways, thou King of saints. Who shall not fear thee, O Lord, and glorify thy name? for thou only art holy: for all nations shall come and worship before thee; for thy judgments are made manifest (Revelation 15:2–4).*

> *And the seven angels came out of the temple, having the seven plagues, clothed in pure and white linen, and having their breasts girded with golden girdles. And one of the four beasts gave unto the seven angels seven golden vials full of the wrath of God, who liveth for*

ever and ever. And the temple was filled with smoke from the glory of God, and from his power; and no man was able to enter into the temple, till the seven plagues of the seven angels were fulfilled. And I heard a great voice out of the temple saying to the seven angels, Go your ways, and pour out the vials of the wrath of God upon the earth (Rev. 15:6–8, 16:1).

The Records of Heaven

The Book of Revelation gives accounts of different groups who are recorded as being in Heaven during this portion of the Tribulation Period and how they arrived there.

Group 1:

And when he had opened the fifth seal, I saw under the altar the souls of them that were slain for the word of God and for the testimony which they held (Rev. 6:9).

These who entered heaven at this time were slain for the Word of God and the testimony which they held. They were given white robes and were told that they should rest until their fellow servants and brethren that should be killed as they were should be fulfilled.

Group 2:

After this I beheld, and, lo, a great multitude, which no man could number, of all nations, and kindreds, and people, and tongues, stood before the throne, and before the Lamb, clothed with white robes, and palms in their hand (Rev. 7:9).

These are now in Heaven and can be ascertained to be those who were martyred as the earlier group (#1) as they also were given white robes and had entered Heaven through martyrdom.

Group 3:

> *And they sang as it were a new song before the throne, and before the four beasts, and the elders: and no man could learn that song but the hundred and forty thousand, which were redeemed from the earth. These were redeemed from among men, being the firstfruits unto God and to the lamb (Rev. 14:3, 4b).*

These 144,000 elected ones are also recorded as being in Heaven before the start of the second half of the Tribulation Period.

In *Revelation 14:9–11*, we see the third angel warning about the consequences of taking the mark of the beast and worshipping his image. Therefore, it can be confirmed that these were in Heaven before the angels were giving out the warning, and are not included among those who overcame the mark of the beast during the second half of the Tribulation Period encompassing Daniel's seventieth week of sevens and the desolation of the antichrist *(Dan. 9:27)*.

There has been quite a bit of discussion concerning the identity of these 144,000 elected ones. It is said that since they are referred to as being chosen from the twelve tribes of Israel that they are Jews. Others seem to think that they refer to a group elected from among all born-again believers. In the apostle Paul's letter to the Hebrews he states:

> *But ye are come unto mount Sion, and unto the city of the living God, the heavenly Jerusalem, and to an innumerable company of angels, to the general*

> *assembly and church of the firstborn which are written*
> *in heaven, and to God the judge of all, and to the*
> *spirits of just men made perfect. And to Jesus the*
> *mediator of the new covenant, and to the blood of*
> *sprinkling, that speaketh better things than that of*
> *Abel (Heb. 12:22–24).*

The above seems to make an interconnection between the two that could indicate that they were the Christians from the Hebrew tribes. Being from the Hebrew tribes does not necessarily mean being from the population of the Jews who are identified as such today but could include all those belonging to the lost tribes of Israel which are scattered worldwide and now are identified as belonging to other nations.

This is the only group for which there is no indication of how they entered Heaven. However, in the account of *Revelation 7:1–4*, it is indicated that while these were being sealed, four angels were standing on the four corners of the earth, holding the four winds of the earth. There therefore is a probability that these were snatched away to Heaven as in a rapture at that time. Having been judged by God to be perfect, they do not require any further testing of their loyalty as those who would be finally tested during the second three-and-one-half-year portion of the antichrist's reign and be beheaded.

Group 4:

> *And I saw as it were a sea of glass mingled with fire:*
> *and them that had gotten the victory over the beast,*
> *and over his image, and over his mark, and over the*
> *number of his name, stand on the sea of glass, having*
> *the harps of God (Rev. 15:2).*

This is the final group who were beheaded for not taking the mark of the beast, nor the number of his name, nor worshipping his image during the second portion of Daniel's seventieth week of sevens during the reign of the antichrist.

It can be determined without doubt that the members of this group were participants of the first resurrection who were raptured at the coming of the Lord.

From these records of the saints in Heaven, it shows that many saints were martyred throughout the Tribulation Period prior to the Day of the Lord and that there will be no pre-tribulation rapture.

The Dead in Christ Shall Rise First

> *For the Lord shall descend from heaven with a shout, with the voice of the archangel, and with the trump of God: and the dead in Christ shall rise first: then we which are alive and remain shall be caught up together with them in the clouds, to meet the Lord in the air: and so shall we ever be with the Lord. Wherefore comfort one another with these words (1 Thess. 4:16–17).*

In the above passage of Scripture, we see that at the coming of the Lord, the dead in Christ will rise first; afterwards, we who are alive and remain shall be caught up together with them in the clouds.

It is important to examine this Scripture in order to understand fully "the dead in Christ shall rise first." Do they include the whole population of saints who have died and are now in Heaven who will return to their graves and be resurrected at the Day of the Lord? Or is there an entirely different suggestion of a first resurrection exclusively for the group (#4) who were beheaded for the witness of Jesus during the second half of the seventieth week of sevens of the Tribulation Period during the reign of the Antichrist?

By the interpreting of Scripture: "For precept must be upon precept, precept upon precept; line upon line, line upon line; here a little, and there a little (Is. 28:10)," we will discover who are the dead in Christ who will rise first.

> *And I saw thrones, and they sat upon them, and judgment was given unto them: and I saw the souls of them that were beheaded for the witness of Jesus, and for the word of God, and which had not worshipped the beast, neither his image, neither had received his mark upon their foreheads, or in their hands; and they lived and reigned with Christ a thousand years. But the rest of the dead lived not again until the thousand years were finished. This is the first resurrection (Rev. 20:4).*

In the above, the apostle John is describing a scene at the start of the new millennium in which satan is shut up for a thousand years. He speaks of something that occurred during the time of the Tribulation Period to the Christians who did not worship the beast or take his mark. They were beheaded and are the dead in Christ who were raised up at the first resurrection at the Day of the Lord.

This Scripture clearly states that this is the first resurrection and that the rest of the dead lived not again until the thousand years were finished. It follows, therefore, that there cannot be another first resurrection occurring at any secret, pre-tribulation rapture.

It can also be determined that the dead in Christ who were resurrected at this first resurrection are not the whole population of saints who had died throughout the entire Christian era; but only those who were still on the earth during the reign of the antichrist and had suffered martyrdom.

Upon death, they were not "absent from the body present with the Lord," but remained until the Day of the Lord to be resurrected from the dead in their earthly bodies. Perhaps, this was because they had to return to the earth to rule and reign during the millennium age.

The timeline for this can be determined to be the period immediately before the appearing of the seven angels with the seven golden vials full of the wrath of God *(Rev. 15:6).*

> *For this we say unto you by the word of the Lord, that we which are alive and remain unto the coming of the Lord shall not prevent them which are asleep (at the coming of the Lord). For the Lord himself shall descend from heaven with a shout, with the voice of the archangel, and with the trump of God: and the dead in Christ shall rise first: then we which are alive and remain shall be caught up together with them in the clouds, to meet the Lord in the air: and so shall we ever be with the Lord (1 Thess. 4: 15–17).*

Reigning and Ruling in the Millennium Age

Traditionally, it was believed that all of the saints would be reigning and ruling with Christ in the millennium age; however, it is indicated that these will consist only of those who were partakers of the first resurrection, overcame and kept His works unto the end and were beheaded. They were the ones who sat upon thrones and to whom judgment was given *(Rev. 20:4).*

> *And he that overcometh, and keepeth my works unto the end, to him will I give power over the nations: and he shall rule them with a rod of iron; as the vessels*

of a potter shall they be broken to shivers: even as I received of my Father (Rev. 2: 26,27).

Blessed and holy is he that hath part in the first resurrection: on such the second death hath no power, but they shall be priests of God and of Christ, and shall reign with him a thousand years (Revelation 20:6).

Christ, the Firstfruits of Them that Slept

But now is Christ risen from the dead and become the firstfruits of them that slept. For since by man came death, by man came also the resurrection of the dead. For as in Adam all die, even so in Christ shall all be made alive. But every man in his own order: Christ the firstfruits; afterward they that are Christ's at his coming (1 Cor. 15:20–23).

It would seem that "But every man in his own order: Christ the firstfruits; afterward they that are Christ's at his coming" indicates that there would be those who will be made alive according to their particular order before those who will be resurrected at the coming of the Lord.

It has been shown in "Records of Heaven" that many of the saints who died during the Tribulation Period were in Heaven after death.

There also have been testimonies by those who had died and were resurrected that upon death they did not sleep in the grave but were immediately taken to their final destination.

In Luke 16:19–31, Jesus gives an account of the rich man and Lazarus. Here it is told that both Lazarus and the rich man did not sleep in the grave but were carried away immediately to their eternal destination.

The Bible also states:

> *Therefore, we are always confident knowing that whilst we are at home in the body, we are absent from the Lord. For we walk by faith not by sight. We are confident, I say, and willing rather to be absent from the body, and to be present with the Lord (2 Cor. 5:6–8).*

> *For as the Father raiseth up the dead, and quickeneth them, even so the Son quickeneth whom He will (John 5:21).*

> *Verily, verily, I say unto you, he that heareth my word, and beliveth on him that sent me, hath everlasting life, and shall not come into condemnation but is passed from death unto life (John. 5:24).*

The passages of Scripture below show that mass resurrections of the dead also will occur:

> *Thy dead men shall live, together with my dead body shall they arise. Awake and sing, ye that dwell in dust: for thy dew is as the dew of herbs, and the earth shall cast out the dead (Isa. 26:19).*

> *Marvel not at this: for the hour is coming, in the which all that are in the graves shall hear His voice, and shall come forth; they that have done good, unto the resurrection of life; and they that done evil, unto the resurrection of damnation (John 5: 28, 29).*

It is written that there also will be another resurrection at the end of the Millennium.

> *But the rest of the dead lived not again until the thousand years were finished (Rev. 20:5a).*

The Victory of the Saints

The tribulation would be a time of horror. Those days will be shortened because of the elect *(Matt. 24:22)*. The Church will be supernaturally protected by God during the first half of the Tribulation Period during the reign of the antichrist. She would be full of the fullness of God and have victory over satan.

> *And to the woman were given two wings of a great eagle, that she might fly into the wilderness, into her place, where she is nourished for a time, and times, and half a time, from the face of the serpent. And the serpent cast out of his mouth water as a flood after the woman, that he might cause her to be carried away of the flood. And the earth helped the woman, and the earth opened her mouth, and swallowed up the flood which the dragon cast out of his mouth And the dragon was wroth with the woman, and went to make war with the remnant of her seed, which keep the commandments of God, and have the testimony of Jesus (Rev.12:14–17).*

Having the testimony of Jesus refers to those who have been born again and could include the Jews as well who will be restored before the Day of the Lord.

> *Repent ye therefore, and be converted, that your sins may be blotted out, when the times of refreshing shall come from the presence of the Lord. And he shall send Jesus Christ, which before was preached unto you: whom the heaven must receive until the times of restitution of all things, which God hath spoken by the mouth of all his holy prophets since the world began (Acts 3: 19–21)*

During the last three-and-one-half years of the Tribulation Period, when the antichrist starts to reign, the saints would be given into his hands by God.

> *And he shall speak great words against the most High, and shall wear out the saints of the most High, and think to change times and laws: and they shall be given into his hand until a time and times and the dividing of time (Dan.7:25).*

> *And it was given unto him to make war with the saints, and to overcome them: and power was given him over all kindreds, and tongues, and nations (Rev.13:7)*

God has a great purpose for this giving over of the saints to the antichrist. These are the ones who would be tested, tried, beheaded, and judged. They would be partakers of the first resurrection and would have proven themselves to be worthy of entering into the Millennium Age to reign with Christ for a thousand years.

> *Blessed and holy is he that hath part in the first resurrection: on such the second death hath no power, but they shall be priests of God and of Christ, and shall reign with him a thousand years (Rev. 20:6).*

There is in the book of Daniel a brief synopsis of the Tribulation Period and the victory of the saints:

> *Thus he said, the fourth beast shall be the fourth kingdom upon earth, which shall be diverse from all kingdoms, and shall devour the whole earth, and shall tread it down, and break it in pieces. And the*

ten horns out of this kingdom are ten kings that shall arise: and another shall rise after them; and he shall be diverse from the first, and he shall subdue three kings. And he shall speak great words against the most High, and shall wear out the saints of the most High, and think to change times and laws: and they shall be given into his hand until a time and times and the dividing of time. But the judgment shall sit, and they shall take away his dominion, to consume and to destroy it unto the end. And the kingdom and dominion, and the greatness of the kingdom under the whole heaven, shall be given to the people of the saints of the most High, whose kingdom is an everlasting kingdom, and all dominions shall serve and obey him.

Hitherto is the end of the matter. As for me Daniel, my cogitations much troubled me, and my countenance changed in me: but I kept the matter in my heart (Dan. 7:23–28).

The Deception of the Church

The Church is being kept in deception about the truth of the Gospel concerning these end-time events. This is a deliberate satanic scheme whose plan it is to have the saints unprepared for the difficult times ahead; it was also being allowed by God for His own sovereign purpose.

This escapism theory in a secret rapture before the Tribulation Period does not bear witness to the general trend of the teachings of the apostle Paul who always taught us to stand and use our mighty weapons. This certainly will be needed during the Tribulation Period.

Finally, my brethren, be strong in the Lord, and in the power of His might. Put on the whole armour of God that ye may be able to stand against the wiles of the devil. For we wrestle not against flesh and blood, but against principalities, against powers, against the rulers of the darkness of this world, against spiritual wickedness in high places. Wherefore take unto you the whole armour of God that ye may be able to withstand in the evil day, and having done all to stand. Stand therefore, having your lions girt about with truth, and having on the breastplate of righteousness; and your feet shod with the preparation of the gospel of peace: Above all, taking the shield of faith wherewith ye shall be able to quench all the fiery darts of the wicked. And take the helmet of salvation, and the sword of the spirit which is the word of God: Praying always with all prayer and supplication in the spirit, and watching thereunto with all perseverance and supplication for all the saints (Eph. 6:10–17).

For though we walk in the flesh, we do not war after the flesh: For the weapons of our warfare are not carnal, but mighty through God to the pulling down of strongholds; casting down imaginations, and everything that exalteth itself against the knowledge of God, and bringing into captivity every thought to the obedience of Christ (2 Cor. 10:3–5).

And they overcame him by the blood of the Lamb and by the word of their testimony; and they loved not their lives unto death (Rev. 12:11).

He which testifieth these things saith, surely I come quickly. Amen. Even so, come, Lord Jesus (Rev. 22:20).

Afterword

I believe that the writing of this book came about as an answer to the prayers of the saints for the cleansing of the Church and for the greater glory.

My part was not praying with them but asking the Lord to answer their prayers. I believed He then used me for conveying this message, which deals with the cleansing of the Church and the end-time glory. This is how it happened.

One morning I woke up to a very bright and sunny day—I even commented on how bright it was—then in a matter of minutes it suddenly became quite dark and I looked through the window to see what was happening.

I was quite awed by what I saw. There on the Cross on the roof of the Catholic Church next door to my home I saw a very large image of Jesus from His head down to His chest, and I saw in His open chest a big bleeding heart. I heard Him say, not audibly but in my spirit: "My heart is bleeding for what is about to befall America. I am going to cleanse My Church." I was also shown something else which I am not allowed to disclose at this time.

Very soon after this, the Lord came to me and told me that He had a task for me to do which was the writing of this book about the cleansing of the Church and the end-time glory.

Isaiah 28 is the key for this cleansing of the Church. There will now be great unity among the many different denominations and cults as everyone will be on the one Foundation Stone laid in Zion.

I received a vision about this. I was sitting at a table on which there was a large black and white paper drawing of an unfinished building on a very solid foundation stone; adjacent to it were many small buildings each on its own foundation. Suddenly, the bricks from the small buildings started flying off the paper, one at a time, and fitting themselves onto the large building with the solid foundation stone.

This shows that the cleansing of the Church from this "Mystery of Iniquity" will also lead to the unity of the Church.

Notes

1. Ice, Dr. Thomas. Excerpt from "Apostasia." Retrieved 24 Apr. 2017. Online posting. <www.pre–trib.org.>
2. Excerpt from "Epistle Dedicatory." Letter from the Translators of the King James Bible to King James. Retrieved 24 Aug. 2018. Online posting. <www.thelostbooks.org.>
3. Clarke, Adam. "Commentary on 2 Thessalonians 2:8. The Adam Clarke Commentary." Retrieved 31 July 2018. Online posting. <htpps://www.studylight.org/commentaries/acc/2–thessalonians–2.html. 1832 >
4. "Martin Luther and the 95 Theses; The Reformation–Facts & Summary." Retrieved 24 Apr. 2018. Online posting. < www. history.com.>

About The Author

Eunice S. Forcet was born again and filled with the Spirit of God in 1989. Since then she has been anointed and appointed to receive revelation messages for those in the Body of Christ who are seeking and asking for the truth of the Scriptures.

This book is an answer to prayer for those who were asking for revelation knowledge about the cleansing of the Church and the outpouring of the end time glory.

Contact information: sillen@bell.net.

www.ingramcontent.com/pod-product-compliance
Lightning Source LLC
Chambersburg PA
CBHW032309070726
47590CB00015B/1466